UNCEASING PRAYER

# Unceasing Prayer

## A BEGINNER'S GUIDE

Debra K. Farrington

PARACLETE PRESS
BREWSTER, MASSACHUSETTS

Unless otherwise designated, Scripture quotations are from the New Revised Standard Version of the Bible, copyright 1989 by the Division of Christian Education of the National Council of the Churches of Christ in the USA. All rights reserved. Used by permission.

Scripture quotations designated KJV are taken from the King James Version of the Bible.

Scripture quotations designated BCP are taken from The Book of Common Prayer, published by The Church Hymnal Corporation, New York, 1979.

The prayers on pages 9, 17, 32, 33, 43, 85, 99, 138 originally appeared in Living Faith Day by Day: How the Sacred Rules of Monastic Tradition Can Help You Live Spiritually in the Modern World. Debra K. Farrington. Published by Perigee Books, New York, 2000.

Library of Congress Cataloging-in-Publication Data:
Farrington, Debra K.
   Unceasing prayer : a beginner's guide / Debra K. Farrington.
      p.     cm.
   ISBN 1-55725-304-8 (pbk.)
   1. Prayer. 2. Prayers. 3. Bible–Prayers. I. Title.
BV215 .F38   2002
242—dc21                         2002007841

10 9 8 7 6 5 4 3 2 1

Published by Paraclete Press
Brewster, Massachusetts
www.paracletepress.com

Printed in the United States of America.

# CONTENTS

# FOREWORD

*And we beseech you, brethren . . .*
*Pray without ceasing. . . .*
*(1 Thessalonians 5:12, 17 KJV)*

Unceasing prayer. The phrase itself conjures. The heart yearns toward it as if toward some bit of misplaced Eden or some moment of play imperfectly remembered from childhood. That such an exercise might once have been possible, that such a commerce between us and him, the human and the divine, might ever have been our lot as creatures is so far beyond most adult Christians' deciphering that we hold its mention at worst as a spiritual tease and at best as a prophetic myth of what might, after death, yet come to be. Either that, or we retreat before the face of its absurdity, labeling it as the domain of the saint, the mystic, the sweetly ordained, and thereby spare ourselves the self-expenditures of engaging faith at so strenuous a level.

It is absolutely true, of course, that by the time we reach adulthood, most of us who are Christian today have used whole skeins of doubt and sloth and fear to bind up and then set aside many of the spiritual possibilities opened to us by our faith. The truth also is, however, that few of those possibilities are ever passed over quite so glibly, so almost unconsciously, as that of unceasing prayer. Unaware of our loss, we fail to mourn it and, therefore, to mourn our own diminishment. The book you are now holding is one contemporary Christian's attempt both to show us the breadth of our ignorance and loss and, having done that, to return us as well to our religious birthright. It is also, by its very nature, a confession of her own faith.

Debra Farrington's is a complex personality, as complex, in fact, as any I have ever known and/or come to love. Her gift, perhaps as a result of living for years with that particular turn of character, is the rare one of pushing complexity over and beyond itself into utter, silent, graceful simplicity. And this is a simple book. Like everything Farrington does, however, it is not so much deceptively so as really so. And as such, it is a dangerous book.

*Unceasing Prayer*, to put the matter another way, constitutes a threat to the spiritual status quo in the religious lives of most of us because it successfully challenges the lazy soul's old defenses or, more charitably, the uninformed soul's former ignorance. For those of us who really like our spiritual lives unencumbered by much interfacing, at least on a routine basis, between the ordinary and the eternal, it will be an especially unsettling book; and even an accomplished Christian who determines to read and reflect here should be forewarned that his or her belief will probably be differently understood (not to mention differently served) as a result of the endeavor.

Farrington's unpretentious call to the constant business of sanctifying the quotidian is, in other words, as disruptive a proposition as it is an historic and apostolic one. I urge you to enter it with caution, therefore, but also with a greedy hope; for the fare Farrington sets before us in this small volume, while it is the substance and means of St. Paul's admonition, is also and by the same token, a fore-taste of Heaven's table.

*Phyllis Tickle*

# ACKNOWLEDGMENTS

Without many people whose vision is clearer than my own, this little book would never have seen the light of day. In a previous book, I talked about these unceasing prayers, and gave a handful of examples, and my friend, Mary Anne Brussat, fell in love with them. She, in turn, told Kathy Kastilahn, at *The Lutheran*, about them, and Kathy was kind enough to publish some of them in that magazine. Their delight in the prayers and the practice they represent encouraged me to write an entire book of them.

I owe thanks as well to Phyllis Tickle, one of my favorite souls in this world, who encouraged me to keep the good parts of the first draft of this book, and delete some of the less wonderful parts. She is a wise woman with a good eye, not to mention one of the great gifts in my life. Thanks, too, to Lil Copan, who edited this book and made wonderful suggestions in a very helpful way. If you ever need a cheering squad, Lil's your woman. I am deeply grateful to Lillian Miao and Carol Showalter at Paraclete, who were willing to take a chance on this little book. They are women I admire deeply, and I am blessed by their friendship. And to all the folks at Paraclete—Jennifer and Christy and the rest of the marketing and sales staff, and to the designer, Lisa

Buckley—thanks for all you do. Without your gifts this book would be much less than it is. And, as always, thanks to Linda Roghaar, my agent, who alternates between being business manager and therapist, and always seems to know which one I need at the moment.

# INTRODUCTION

*The call to unceasing prayer is not an
invitation to divided consciousness; it does not
imply that we pay any less attention to daily
realities or retreat from life's responsibilities. . . .
[It] means being consciously constantly
conscious of the presence of God amidst the
changing complexion of everyday life.*[1]

> In the Spirit of Happiness,
> *The Monks of New Skete*

Many years ago, in a small shop,
a plaque caught my eye. "Thy word
have I hidden in mine heart," it said,
quoting one version of lines from
Psalm 119. I was drawn to the
words, but truthfully, I bought the
plaque more for its simple beauty.
Little did I understand the prophetic
wisdom of the words, that the tradition of hiding God's words in my

heart—of praying without ceasing—would become part of my life.

If you had asked me what praying without ceasing was at that time, I would not have connected it with anything in my own life. Your own associations are probably similar to my early ones. When you picture yourself praying without ceasing, perhaps you see yourself alone in a desert cave praying from sunrise to sunset, like the early Christian hermits. Maybe, on the other hand, you have spent time with Eastern traditions, and you imagine yourself sitting cross-legged, quietly reciting a mantra over and over again. In all likelihood, you don't see yourself doing the dishes, feeding the cat, working at your desk, making love, or helping the kids with their homework. Yet all of these activities—and everything else we do during the day—are opportunities for acknowledging God's presence. When we take even the smallest moment to notice the presence of God in the midst of daily life, we are praying. When we begin to do that often during the day, we are praying without ceasing. We are, as the Monks of New Skete write, becoming "consciously constantly conscious of the presence of God."

Every generation seems to discover this kind of everyday spirituality anew, but the practice of purposefully remembering and acknowledging God's presence in our daily activities has existed in world religions since our earliest memories. The various faiths each found their own way of recognizing the presence of God. The Book of Leviticus and other early books of the Bible contain a record of the laws the Jews observed in faith-fulness to God. Dietary practices, Sabbath-keeping, and rituals around common events such as intercourse and menstruation acknowledged God's presence and action in the everyday and are still practiced by observant Jews today. In ancient times and continuing to the present, simple daily activities—such as washing one's hands before a meal—have been ways for Jews to recognize and express gratitude for God in their midst.

Another ancient faith, Islam, has a regular practice of brief prayers, called *dhikrs*, that Muslims use to remind themselves to focus on God throughout the day. *Dhikrs*, or invo-cations as the word is translated, are short phrases, primarily from the Sufi tradition, that employ one of the

Arabic names for God drawn from the Qur'an. The object of speaking a *dhikr* (which might be a prayer as simple as "Praise belongs to God") is to remember God throughout the day, as commanded by the revelations of the prophets.

Buddhists, too, have brief prayers, called *gathas,* to help them remain in the present moment. These one- or two-line prayers or vows help Buddhists become more conscious of what they are doing at a particular moment, and heighten their awareness of what is occurring now, rather than what happened yesterday or what may happen tomorrow. The Buddhist tradition varies from the Jewish and Islamic ones in that it does not focus on God, but all three traditions value the importance of returning to a spiritual focus often during one's daily activities.

*Debra K. Farrington* xxiii

The tradition of praying without ceasing has also been a part of Christian practice since its earliest days. Paul's First Letter to the Thessalonians urged the Thessalonians to pray without ceasing as one part of leading the Christian life. This particular instruction is nested in a list of others:

> But we appeal to you, brothers and sisters, to respect those who labor among you, and have charge of you in the Lord and admonish you; esteem them very highly in love because of their work. Be at peace among yourselves. And we urge you, beloved, to admonish the idlers, encourage the faint hearted, help the weak, be patient with all of them. See that none of you repays evil for evil, but always seek to do good to one another and to all.

Rejoice always, pray without ceasing, give thanks in all circumstances; for this is the will of God in Christ Jesus for you. Do not quench the Spirit. Do not despise the words of prophets, but test everything; hold fast to what is good; abstain from every form of evil (1 Thessalonians 5:12-22).

This ancient list, highlighting many of the ways in which we honor and call upon God's presence in our daily lives, sounds remarkably contemporary. Respecting those we work with, listening to those who criticize us, encouraging and helping others, seeking to do good, giving thanks, being joyful, were then, and continue to be, opportunities for prayer throughout the day.

As we have rediscovered in recent years, the Celtic peoples

understood this very clearly. They believed that God accompanied them every moment of the day and night, and they used short blessings and prayers to acknowledge or call upon God as they performed their chores. There were prayers for lighting the fire in the morning and extinguishing it at night. Prayers accompanied milking the cows, making butter, weaving, herding the animals, and all other activities. Esther de Waal, a noted Celtic scholar, writes of their prayers: "They are the prayers of a people who are so busy from dawn to dusk, from dark to dark, that they have little time for long, formal prayers. Instead throughout the day they do whatever has to be done carefully, giving it their full attention, yet at the same time making it the occasion for prayer."[2]

De Waal's description of the Celts fits many of our lives today. So many of us are busy from dawn to dusk, with little time for formal prayer, so perhaps it is no surprise that we are rediscovering ancient traditions for praying as the day and night move along. I realized this for myself a few years ago. One morning in the shower I found myself repeating the lines from Psalm 51: "Create in me a clean heart, O God." An activity as ordinary as a shower had prompted me to ask God to cleanse my soul while I washed my body. Over the next while I observed myself stopping momentarily to thank or acknowledge God or to ask for help as I went about the normal activities of my life. I would notice the beauty of the morning, and remember that God had made the day. Petting the cat was a reminder of the trust God had placed in me, by giving me another creature to care for. None of these brief prayers interrupted the activity in which I was engaged at the time, nor were they even conscious decisions to pray. Each was simply a spontaneous response to, or recollection of, God's presence in my day. Finally, I realized that these were prayer times, just as much as any formal ones I set aside. My daily activities became my pointers—my teachers—that reminded me of God's hand in all that I do.

It is easy enough for most of us to remember God during formal prayer times, corporate worship, or during the holy days of the church calendar. But this book of Scripture-prayers is about doing that throughout all of our days and nights. These prayers do not invoke the presence of God; God is with us 24/7. God does not ever forget us for a moment, but we forget God regularly. We neglect to offer thanks and praise, to confess our meanness of spirit and our mistakes. We too easily focus on ourselves, and forget to pray for the needs of others, or to bless the world around us. We rely too heavily on our own resources, and don't ask—or listen for—God's guidance along life's path. In short, we put ourselves, rather than God, at the center of our universe and our vision becomes skewed.

I hope that this book of short Scripture-prayers will invite you to pray all day long as a way of remembering and expressing gratitude for God's presence in your life. Some of the prayers thank God or ask for help, while others are statements to help you affirm that God is present and acting in your life. Many are addressed to God directly, and some of the Scriptures have been slightly adapted to make them into prayers, rather than statements. Other Scriptures are more like statements or reminders that God is operating in our lives and everything around us. They're meant to help you remember that God is with you at all moments, even when you forget to talk to God directly. The prayers and thoughts in part one of the book relate to the normal events of most days, and the ones in the second part to more generalized needs, such as moments when help or guidance is needed. Memorize the Scriptures that speak most powerfully to you if you wish. But the prayers given here are meant to be catalysts to your own prayers. They're just words and ideas to get you started. So feel free to explore Scripture further for other ideas, or to use your imagination and words of your own to talk with God.

All of the prayers in this book come from the Bible, and some may surprise you. They were written centuries ago, at a time when e-mail and other technological wonders were not even imagined, so you may find yourself marveling at how much these ancient words still have to say to us today. Most of all, I hope they will deepen your awareness of God's presence in your own life, for the ancient Celts were quite right: Everything that occurs in our world is an opportunity for prayer. May the Scripture-prayers you read here invite you to pray, as our ancestors did, unceasing prayers.

*Debra K. Farrington*

# Part One

# 1

## *This Is the Day the Lord Has Made*

GREETING THE NEW DAY

Mornings are the easiest time of the day for me to remember God's presence. Some of that is because I'm a morning person and I wake up ready to go most days, so if you're a night person, you'll have to forgive my enthusiasm for the light of a new day. But, unless I've been fretting about something in my sleep all night and wake with that on my mind, God is usually the first thing I think about each morning.

Mornings, in most faith traditions, have traditionally been a time for prayers and for praising God. Perhaps—even unconsciously—we wake up relieved that God has brought us to yet another day. "Surely it is God who saves me," reads Isaiah 12:2 in *The Book of Common Prayer*, a standard reading for morning prayer. Each morning is a small resurrection. Having awakened for yet another day, it is natural to want to praise God. "Lord, open our lips, and our mouth shall proclaim your praise," many people say as part of the morning prayers that have come down to us over the centuries.

In the morning we can also take the time to invite God to be a part of our day, and to count our blessings. I frequently greet the new day by looking out at my small garden and the neighborhood around me, with a prayer of thankfulness for all of it, even when I've had a bad night's sleep and I'm grumpy or irritated. That God has brought me to yet another day, full of possibilities, is always worthy of praise.

*Arise, shine;*
*for our light has come, and*
*the glory of the LORD has*
*risen upon us.*

*from* ISAIAH 60:1

IN THANKFULNESS FOR GOD'S
PRESENCE FROM SUNRISE
TO SUNSET

*I bless God the* LORD,
*who speaks*
*and summons the earth*
*from the rising of the sun*
*to its setting.*

*from* PSALM 50:1

*Satisfy us in the morning*
*with your steadfast love,*
*so that we may rejoice*
*and be glad all our days.*

PSALM 90:14

*This*
*is the day*
*that the Lord has made;*
*let us rejoice*
*and be glad in it.*

PSALM 118:24

*O Lord,*
*open my lips,*
*and my mouth will declare*
*your praise.*

PSALM 51:15

*Every day
I will bless you,
and praise your name
forever and ever.*

PSALM 145:2

# 2

## *Create in Me a Clean Heart*

PREPARING FOR THE DAY AHEAD

You probably don't think about brushing your teeth as an opportunity for praying. In part, that's because of our Christian heritage. Christians, through the centuries, have struggled with the relationship of our bodies with our spiritual lives. There have been times in our history when good and faithful men and women believed that the more they denied the body's needs, the closer their souls were to God. This understanding carried through the generations and influenced our understandings about sexuality, and about our physicality itself. But the fact that Jesus came to us as a man with a human body that had the same needs as our bodies have, and that he took the bodily needs of others seriously, suggests that bodies are important and good, rather than hindrances to our souls.

Bodies, minds, and souls cannot actually be separated from one another. I find, for instance, that my prayer life is less focused and vibrant when I'm tired or when I haven't exercised regularly. Pain in my back, which comes from being too stationary, effects how well I am able to think and do my job. Body, mind, and soul are all pieces of the whole. Failing to care for one part of that whole negatively affects all the parts.

Our bodies, and all of the needs of our bodies, are a gift from God, and we are the stewards of that gift. Too often we have been taught that taking care of ourselves, or noticing our body's concerns, is selfish or self-centered. Though we can take attention to our bodies to selfish extremes, basic and conscientious care is an important spiritual act, one that acknowledges and cares for the gift we have received. While we tend to our physical needs, we can be mindful of the One who gave us this body in the first place, and reflect on the correspondence between what we do to care for ourselves and what God does to care for us.

*I am
God's temple
and God's Spirit dwells
in me.*

*from* 1 CORINTHIANS 3:16

*Create in me a clean heart,*
*O God, and put a new*
*and right spirit within me.*

PSALM 51:10

*Those who have
clean hands and
pure hearts . . .
will receive blessing
from the LORD.*

PSALM 24:4–5

*Let me,*
*with ears to hear,*
*listen!*

*from* MARK 4:9

*As for me,*
*I shall behold your face*
*in righteousness;*
*when I awake*
*I shall be satisfied,*
*beholding your likeness.*

PSALM 17:15

*Even*
*the hairs of my head*
*are all counted.*

*from* LUKE 12:7

*Set a guard*
*over my mouth,*
*O LORD;*
*keep watch over*
*the door of my lips.*

PSALM 141:3

*As one
of God's chosen ones,
holy and beloved,
clothe me with
compassion, kindness,
humility, meekness,
and patience.*

*from* COLOSSIANS 3:12

*My soul
thirsts for God,
for the living God.*

PSALM 42:2

*He will feed his flock*
*like a shepherd.*

ISAIAH 40:11

# 3

## *All My Works Praise You, O Lord*

PRAYERS FOR THE DAY'S WORK

Before the revival in interest in Celtic spirituality in the last decade or so, praying while working would probably have struck us as a bit odd. Thanks to those who have taught us in recent years about our Celtic heritage, we have discovered that the practice of noticing God's presence, even in our daily tasks, is an ancient and revered practice. The Celts had prayers for stoking the fire in the morning, for herding the animals,

27

for blessing the kitchen before cooking, and many other ordinary activities of their day. God was found in the details of the mundane in their world, not just in churches on Sunday.

The theme of prayer in the midst of ordinary chores also found expression in some of the later Christian literature. *The Practice of the Presence of God*, written by Brother Lawrence at the end of the seventeenth century, explored what it meant to be continually aware of God's presence. The Abbé of Beaufort wrote that Brother Lawrence "found no more excellent means of going to God than the ordinary actions prescribed to him by obedience. . . . It is a grave error to believe that fixed prayer times are different from any other time, for we are as strictly obliged to be united to God through our duties in their appropriate time as by prayer in its time."[3] And so Brother Lawrence practiced prayer and contemplation of God while working in the kitchen or in the shoe repair shop, just as he did in the chapel.

Noticing and giving thanks for God's presence while we work—whether that be work outside the home or work that we do at home—can take a bit of practice. We live in a culture that tells us that we should "be all you can be" and that worships accomplishment, not as the hand or gift of God, but as the unassisted success of an individual. Work spaces, more often than not, do not feel like worship spaces, but that is because we define worship spaces so narrowly. God fills our kitchens, bathrooms, offices, and all our work sites just as fully as God inhabits a sanctuary. Whatever work we are doing, be it paid or unpaid, we are acting as God's hands in the world, as this prayer from *The Book of Common Prayer* reminds us:

Almighty God, our heavenly Father, you declare your glory and show forth your handiwork in the heavens and in the earth: Deliver us in our various occupations from the service of self alone, that we may do the work you give us to do in truth and beauty and for the common good; for the sake of him who came among us as one who serves, your Son Jesus Christ our Lord, who lives and reigns with you and the Holy Spirit, one God, for ever and ever. Amen.

We can take many opportunities to pray for or about our work. If we commute to work, we can use that time to pray for guidance and to examine whether or not we are answering God's call for us with the work we do. At the beginning of our shift or task, we can ask God's blessing on what needs to be done. Throughout the day we can take time to be aware of God's presence in a meeting or an encounter at the grocery store, to seek God's will, or to thank God for what has been accomplished and for giving us work to do in the first place. Recognizing God's presence in our work, and thanking God for what gets accomplished reminds us that we serve God and prevents us from making work—rather than God— the center of our existence.

*Debra K. Farrington*   31

*Make me*
*to know your ways,*
*O LORD;*
*teach me your paths.*

PSALM 25:4

*Let the favor
of the LORD our God
be upon us,
and prosper for us
the work of our hands.*

PSALM 90:17

*Whatever my task,*
*I will put myself into it,*
*as it is done for the Lord.*

*from* COLOSSIANS 3:23

*I will
sprinkle clean water
upon you,
and you shall be clean
from all your uncleannesses,
and from all your idols
I will cleanse you.*

EZEKIEL 36:25

*Unless
the LORD builds the house,
we who build it
labor in vain.*

*from* PSALM 127:1

## WHEN ANSWERING THE PHONE
## OR AN E-MAIL

*To make an apt answer*
*is a joy to anyone,*
*and a word in season,*
*how good it is.*

PROVERBS 15:23

*Let the words*
*of my mouth*
*and the meditation*
*of my heart*
*be acceptable to you,*
*O LORD,*
*my rock*
*and my redeemer.*

PSALM 19:14

*O LORD,
be gracious to us;
we wait for you.*

ISAIAH 33:2

*I brought nothing
into the world,
so that I can take nothing
out of it;
but if I have food
and clothing,
I will be content with these.*

*from* 1 TIMOTHY 6:7–8

*Lord,*
*visit the earth*
*and water it;*
*you greatly enrich it.*

*from* PSALM 65:9

*May we, who walked in darkness, see a great light.*

*from* ISAIAH 9:2A

*All your works praise you,
O LORD, and your faithful
servants bless you.*

*from* PSALM 145:10

4

# *May Our Mouths Be Filled with Laughter*

PRAYERS FOR LEISURE TIMES

Praying while playing comes hard to me. My sixth grade report card said that I was "little Miss Responsibility herself." Perhaps that came from being the oldest child in a family of four children. I always felt that there was work to be done, and that play was a luxury I usually couldn't afford. This kind of thinking, however, inevitably leads to working too hard, and I bought what we think of as the Protestant

Work Ethic hook, line, and sinker. Luckily, I have a very wise spiritual director who helped me to see the world another way. One June, when I was completely burned out with the work load of the time—and that included my spiritual "to do" list which was just as demanding as my job—my director told me that she wanted me to stop praying for the summer, and make play my prayer. I had absolutely no idea what she was talking about.

Over the course of that summer I made time for leisure and for fun. I began to learn to see my work as something other than a life and death concern each day. I made time to go to ball games, and read books just for fun, and I planted a garden for the first time. Not too far into the summer I found myself breathing deeply and relaxing, laughing, and having fun. And in the process I discovered that God doesn't need me to be deadly serious all the time, that God enjoys my laughter and the creativity that flows from me when I don't take myself so seriously. By the end of the summer I returned to many of my spiritual practices, but I did so because I missed them, rather than because they were things to be accomplished each day.

All of our leisure activities—our hobbies, the things we do to relax and to express our creativity—can be sacred times, times to remember and enjoy the presence of God and to be grateful for our gifts. Planting flowers or repotting houseplants leads us to reflect on protecting and nourishing our own fragile roots, and those of others. Reading a book is an opportunity to discover wisdom from someone else's perspective, to expand our horizons, and perhaps learn to know God from a new vantage point. Gratitude for the gifts we have, or for the giftedness of others, arises naturally as we sing or hum, or applaud a fine performance. The peacefulness or the energy that these activities give us, the sheer enjoyment that we find in participating in them, make leisure times one of the easiest times to pray our prayers of thankfulness to God, the source of all that exists.

*May your word*
*be a lamp to my feet*
*and a light to my path.*

*from* PSALM 119:105

*I am my beloved's,*
*and his desire is for me.*

SONG OF SONGS 7:10

*Those who are planted*
*in the house of the Lord*
*shall flourish*
*in the courts of our God.*

PSALM 92:12 BCP

*In the shadow of your wings
I sing for joy.*

PSALM 63:7B

*May our mouths be filled
with laughter, and our
tongues with shouts of joy.*

*from* PSALM 126:2

*Clap your hands,*
*all you peoples;*
*shout to God*
*with loud songs of joy.*

PSALM 47:1

*May I remember that it was you who formed my inward parts; you knit me together in my mother's womb.*

*from* PSALM 139:13

*Teach me your way,*
*O LORD,*
*that I may walk*
*in your truth.*

PSALM 86:11

*You gave me a wide place*
*for my steps under me,*
*and I am thankful*
*that my feet did not slip.*

*from* PSALM 18:36

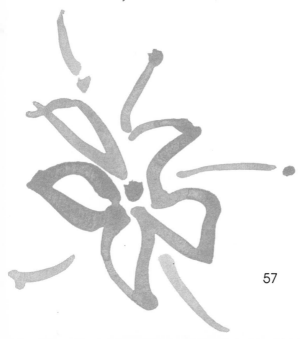

57

# 5

*The Lord
Keep Your Going Out
and Coming In*

PRAYERS OF GREETING AND FAREWELL

Greetings and farewells, beginnings and endings, are perfect moments for acknowledging God's presence, particularly since God is the ultimate beginning and ending. "'I am the Alpha and the Omega,' says the Lord God, who is and who was and who is to come, the Almighty" (Revelation 1:8). Some of these greetings and farewells will be little and routine comings and goings. We leave for work in the morning, or head to the grocery store. We come home at the end of the workday, or we kiss the children goodnight. Other times the beginning or ending will be momentous. A child leaves home to go to college, or we take a loved one to the hospital. All of these moments—big or small—are opportunities to notice God's presence.

To greet someone, or something, properly, is actively to look for and recognize the face of God within the people or the places you come across, and to wish God's blessing on the encounter. Consequently, we can pray that our "hellos" be filled with graciousness, peacefulness, and helpfulness. We greet not only people, but our homes, and other places.

Even opening doors and turning on lights are opportunities for reflecting on God's presence and God's actions in our lives, for giving thanks.

We can take leave of these same people or places in a similar spirit— recognizing the sacred nature of the encounter, noting how it has changed us or what it has promised us, realizing that we will miss it, and blessing it as we go. We leave the house, or we leave home for a period, knowing that God goes with us, guides us, and cares for us. We say goodbye or goodnight to those we care for, and silently, or aloud, ask God to bless and keep these dear people.

*Greetings, favored one!*
*May the Lord be with you.*

*from* LUKE 1:28

*Happy am I*
*who lives in your house,*
*ever singing your praise.*

*from* PSALM 84:4

*May we welcome
one another,
therefore,
just as Christ
has welcomed us,
for the glory of God.*

*from* ROMANS 15:7

## BEFORE LEAVING HOME
## ON A LENGTHY TRIP

*I know*
*that you are with me*
*and will keep me*
*wherever I go,*
*and will bring me back*
*to this land.*

*from* GENESIS 28:15A

*The LORD*
*keep your going out*
*and your coming in*
*from this time on*
*and forevermore.*

*from* PSALM 121:8

*The LORD bless you
and keep you.*

NUMBERS 6:24

*The grace*
*of the Lord Jesus Christ,*
*the love of God,*
*and the communion*
*of the Holy Spirit*
*be with all of you.*

2 CORINTHIANS 13:13

# *Be Still and Know That I Am God*

PRAYERS FOR TIMES OF REST

I used to think that being too busy and focusing too much on productivity was a problem of the late twentieth century, and then I read some books that complained about the same problems more than two hundred years ago. Maybe that's always been the human predicament. I fall into being too busy as easily as the next person does. All around me I see people in airports working on their laptops, while others walk briskly between appointments making as many calls as they can on their cell phone. I hate to admit it, but I can't even schedule an appointment in my day without checking two calendars. Something in us seems to feel we have to be productive absolutely everywhere and at every moment of the day, and maybe of the evening too.

It has become almost a sin to be unproductive, to be out of reach of customers and colleagues, even on vacations. Sometimes the financial need is real—it is extremely difficult for families to survive on a single income today. But at other times, I suspect, we have just gotten into the habit of working too hard, and it is just our pride or our desire to be indispensable that keeps us from resting and relaxing. We forget that even God only worked six days, and then God rested.

So, if God rested on the seventh day, who can blame us for needing to rest much more often than that? We live in physical bodies that need down time, and we have minds that function better with a little time away from the workload. To deny that—to try to keep in constant motion—is to try to outdo God. "It is in vain that you rise up early and go late to rest, eating the bread of anxious toil," we are told in Psalm 127. Naps during the day, days off, and vacations provide us with perspective and energy, and are excellent opportunities for noticing God's presence, for recognizing our limits as human beings, and for being grateful for the gift of rest.

*Be still,
and know that I am God.*

PSALM 46:10A

*The LORD
is my shepherd,
I shall not want.
He makes me lie down
in green pastures;
he leads me
beside still waters;
he restores my soul.*

PSALM 23:1–3A

*I lie down and sleep;*
*I wake again, for you, God,*
*sustain me.*

*from* PSALM 3:5

*Come to me,*
*all you that are weary*
*and are carrying*
*heavy burdens,*
*and I will give you rest.*

MATTHEW 11:28

*In returning and rest
I shall be saved;
in quietness and in trust
shall be my strength.*

*from* ISAIAH 30:15

*Blessed be the LORD,
who has given rest to his
people Israel according to all
that he promised.*

1 KINGS 8:56A

# 7

## *My Soul Yearns for You in the Night*

PRAYERS FOR BEDTIME

I know some people who can drop off to sleep at night within minutes. And I know others who put off going to bed for hours each night because they just can't quite give up the reins of control. The night, and the darkness, can be scary. We cannot control our dreams, and unless we're the parent of a young child who might call us in the night, we're often unaware of what may be happening around us.

To go to sleep is, for many, an act of trust. That's the reason many evening prayer services include a traditional prayer that begins with the line: "Keep watch, dear Lord. . . . "

So the evening is a time for looking back over the day, and counting our blessings. Before we sink into the darkness of sleep, it is wise to reflect on those things that we wish we hadn't done, or on those things that we left undone that day, and give these over to God and ask for forgiveness. An old adage counsels married couples not to go to bed angry. It is the same with our relationship to God; it is wise to clear the air before going to bed.

At nighttime we let go of any control we normally exercise during the daytime, and give ourselves over to darkness in confidence or hopefulness that God will be with us and guide us safely through the nighttime hours. That gives us confidence to release ourselves into God's care for the night, and can even make us bold enough to ask for guidance while we sleep. I have often gleaned tremendous insight from my dreams, particularly on nights when I've prayed for guidance before going to sleep.

On some nights, however, I struggle to let go of the day's activities, and battle with insomnia. Rather than let my mind continue to agonize over the day's events, or tomorrow's anxieties, or whatever is keeping me awake, I have learned to make those hours ones of prayer and watchfulness. That doesn't always bring sleep on as soon as I'd like, but it does help to reduce my stress levels.

And, unlike calling on human friends at that hour, God is never asleep and never seems to mind the company, even at 3 AM.

*Let my prayer*
*be counted as incense*
*before you,*
*and the lifting up*
*of my hands*
*as an evening sacrifice.*

PSALM 141:2

*It is in vain that I rise up early and go late to rest, eating the bread of anxious toil; for God gives sleep to me, his beloved.*

*from* PSALM 127:2

*I bless the LORD*
*who gives me counsel;*
*in the night also*
*my heart instructs me.*

PSALM 16:7

*My soul yearns for you
in the night,
my spirit within me
earnestly seeks you.*

ISAIAH 26:9

*I will both lie down
and sleep in peace;
for you alone, O LORD,
make me lie down in safety.*

PSALM 4:8

*Father, into your hands
I commend my
spirit.*

LUKE 23:46

*My soul
waits for the LORD
more than those who watch
for the morning,
more than those who watch
for the morning.*

PSALM 130:6

# Part Two

8

# My Help
# Comes from the Lord

PRAYERS WHEN YOU NEED HELP

Praying for help when we are distressed or in trouble is both one of the most natural things to do, and one of the most difficult. There is an instinctive need, probably left over from our childhoods, to instantly want to cry out for assistance. "O LORD, make haste to help me," writes the Psalmist several times, and that is our cry too. Each and every day provides us with no end of opportunities to ask for help. The temptations we face, the moments when we're at the end of our rope and patience is gone, even just the small frustrations of waiting in line, are all good opportunities for a short prayer.

Of course, not only do we want help, but we want it now. If I had my way, help would not only be available now, but I would be able to dictate the terms of that assistance as well. Most of us would like to be able to tell God exactly what help we need, how we want it delivered, and what the most convenient delivery time might be. And there's absolutely nothing wrong with asking God for just exactly what we think we need. The difficult part is that sometimes the answer—the assistance God provides—is different from what we had in mind. We ask for guidance while considering two career options, and God suggests a third instead. We beg to be relieved of living through a difficult illness or situation, and instead we are given strength to bear the pain. And, perhaps most difficult, sometimes it seems as if there is no answer at all to our request.

To ask God for help, then, requires courage on our part, and a willingness to be open to whatever response we receive, even apparent silence. We need confidence, too, to keep asking for what we believe we need, to be in conversation with God, knowing that the dialogue will eventually bring clarity.

*My help
comes from the LORD,
who made heaven and earth.*

PSALM 121:2

*I rise before dawn
and cry for help;
I put my hope in your
words.*

PSALM 119:147

97

*Put away from me
crooked speech,
and put devious talk
far from me.*

*from* PROVERBS 4:24

*For your name's sake,*
*O LORD, pardon my guilt,*
*for it is great.*

PSALM 25:11

*When I pass through the
waters, God, you will
be with me; and through the
rivers, they shall not
overwhelm me; when I walk
through fire I shall not be
burned, and the flame shall
not consume me.*

*from* ISAIAH 43:2

*O LORD my God,*
*in you I take refuge;*
*save me from*
*all my pursuers,*
*and deliver me.*

PSALM 7:1

*O LORD, heal me.*

PSALM 6:2

*Glory to you, God,*
*whose power, working in us,*
*can do infinitely more*
*than we can ask or imagine.*

EPHESIANS 3:20 BCP

*Evening and morning*
*and at noon*
*I utter my complaint*
*and moan,*
*and know that*
*You will hear my voice.*

*from* PSALM 55:17

*God be my refuge
and strength,
a very present help in trouble.*

*from* PSALM 46:1

*Do not be far from me,*
*for trouble is near*
*and there is no one to help.*

PSALM 22:11

*My soul is satisfied
as with a rich feast, and my
mouth praises you
with joyful lips...
for you have been my help,
and in the shadow
of your wings
I sing for joy.*

PSALM 63:5,7

# 9

## *Lord, Be Near to the Broken Hearted*

PRAYERS WHEN OTHERS NEED HELP

Recently a friend of mine gave me a ride home from work in a bad snowstorm. It had been snowing for many hours, so the road crews had not been able to do much to clear even the main roads, much less the side streets. Even small hills were a major challenge, and I was truly fearful for the rest of my friend's journey home. I made him promise to call me when he got home so there would be—hopefully—an end to my worrying about his safety that evening. But between the time he dropped me off and the time he called, I found myself in constant prayer. There was absolutely nothing else I could do while waiting but to pray fervently for his safety, and for that of all the others who were on the road that slippery evening.

If we have our eyes and hearts open, there are many who need our prayers each day. Just reading the newspaper or watching the evening news provides ample opportunity for intercessory prayers—prayers on behalf of others. Nightly we hear of violence on our streets or somewhere else, of natural disasters that shake the lives of individuals and communities, and a host of political and economic issues that need our prayerful attention. National events in the wake of the terrorist attacks in September 2001 made many of us more aware of how much others need our prayers. In the course of most days we encounter in person the need of others. Friends, colleagues, and strangers are in need of some kind of help.

We can easily become overwhelmed by the needs and demands of others, especially those that find us helpless to actually offer a cure or solution. It is important to do what we can to help, using whatever resources we have at our disposal. But even when we can do very little else to help, we can hold the concerns of others in our prayers. We can pray that those who need God's help and guidance will be able to be open to God's presence and assistance in their lives.

*Debra K. Farrington* 111

*May the L*ORD* answer you
in the day of trouble.*

*from* PSALM 20:1

*Our souls wait for you
LORD; be our help and shield.*

*from* PSALM 33:20

*LORD, be near
to the brokenhearted, and
save the crushed in spirit.*

*from* PSALM 34:18

*I honor you, L*ORD
*with my substance
and with the first fruits
of all my produce.*

*from* PROVERBS 3:9

*Those who oppress the poor.*
*insult their Maker,*
*but those who are kind*
*to the needy honor him.*

PROVERBS 14:31

*Your eyes, my God,
are in every place,
keeping watch on the evil
and the good.*

*from* PROVERBS 15:3

*Be merciful to us,
O God, be merciful to us,
for in you our souls take
refuge; in the shadow of your
wings we will take refuge,
until the destroying storms
pass by.*

*from* PSALM 57:1

*Save us,
O LORD our God,
and gather us
from among the nations,
that we may give thanks
to your holy name
and glory in your praise.*

PSALM 106:47

*What does
the LORD require of me
but to do justice,
and to love kind-
ness,
and to walk
humbly
with my God?*

*from* MICAH 6:8

## WHEN SOMEONE NEEDS AN ASSURANCE OF GOD'S PRESENCE

*Before you call*
*God will answer,*
*while you are yet speaking*
*God will hear.*

*from* ISAIAH 65:24

# 10

## *O Send Out Your Light and Your Truth*

PRAYERS FOR GUIDANCE

Life is circular. When we are very young—infants and toddlers—we rely on our parents for everything. They are the ones who supply all our needs, including guidance for living. From them we learn not to put our hands on hot burners, or to cross the street without looking both ways. Later, we become teenagers and start declaring our independence from our parents. Guidance, from just about any adult, is frequently unwelcome.

But the older we get, if we become wise at all, the more we discover that we actually do need guidance. Life conspires to remind us that we can't do it all for ourselves, that God is ultimately our true guide, and we are foolish when we fail to listen for what God calls us to do and be. Catholic priest Adrian Van Kaam tells about a nine year "detour" he took as a result of not listening very carefully for God's will. His calling to help others in spiritual development got sidetracked by a nine-year stint developing a program of psychology. He calls that time a confusing one, a period during which he was "unable to listen fully to God's guidance."[4] God doesn't punish us for not listening, for not following, but I've found that living in a way that is outside of what God calls me to be or do is a lot like walking through deep mud. It can be done, but it requires lots of effort.

Life is full of opportunities to pray for guidance. Sometimes we come to a major crossroad—a career or relationship decision, or anything else that requires a major change in our life circumstances—and we spend most of our energy asking for and trying to listen for God's will. But even simple ordinary events, such as a meeting at work, a trying situation, choosing a volunteer project, are good times for pausing to ask God to light the way a little more clearly.

*You are indeed my rock
and my fortress;
for your name's sake lead me
and guide me.*

PSALM 31:3

*You desire truth
in the inward being;
therefore teach me wisdom
in my secret heart.*

PSALM 51:6

*O send out your light
and your truth;
let them lead me;
let them bring me
to your holy hill
and to your dwelling.*

PSALM 43:3

## PRAYER FOR GUIDANCE BEFORE
## A MEETING

*May I delight
to do your will,
O my God;
may your law be
within my heart.*

PSALM 40:8

*I will be still
before the LORD,
and wait patiently for him.*

*from* PSALM 37:7A

*I call upon you,*
*for you will answer me,*
*O God;*
*incline your ear to me,*
*hear my words.*

PSALM 17:6

*Not my will
but yours be done.*

LUKE 22:42B

*How precious
is your steadfast love,
O God! For with you
is the fountain of life;
in your light we see light.*

PSALM 36:7,9

# 11

## O Give Thanks to the Lord

PRAYERS OF GRATITUDE AND CELEBRATION

When you were a little child you were probably like me, and learned that if you really wanted something it was wise to add the word "please" to your request, and then to say "thank you" when you got what you wanted. Our prayers of gratitude throughout the day are our "thank yous" to God, not only for the wonderful people and events that come our way, but sometimes even for the lessons and difficulties. I worked at a

135

consortium of seminaries for many years, and a standard joke was called the "seminarian's prayer," which was: "Lord, save me from yet another learning experience." While difficult moments can be painful or stressful, there are some that help us grow or gain skills, and perhaps somewhere along the way we can give thanks even for those things that initially seem like obstacles in our path.

An attitude of gratitude can also help us stay focused on the blessings that are ours. It is easy to be thankful in the midst of a birthday party, anniversary celebration, or holiday. But our gratitude to God is equally important in the midst of busy days, even those that are stressful or difficult and when we're more focused on how frustrated or tired we are. I am not suggesting that we belittle the feelings of fatigue, irritation, or any other feelings; we don't need to whitewash everything and pretend that all is well. God knows what we're feeling, whether we like it or not. But we can achieve a more balanced life and perspective by regularly remembering the people, events, and gifts in our life that bring us joy, and consciously thanking God for those blessings.

*Blessed be the LORD,
the God of Israel, who alone
does wondrous things.*

PSALM 72:18

*O give thanks to the LORD, for he is good; his steadfast love endures forever.*

PSALM 118:1

*The LORD*
*is my strength*
*and my shield;*
*in him my heart trusts;*
*so I am helped,*
*and my heart exults,*
*and with my song*
*I give thanks to him.*

PSALM 28:7

140

## AFTER BEING HAPPILY SURPRISED

*Surely the* LORD
*is in this place—*
*and I did not know it.*

GENESIS 28:16B

*Some friends
play at friendship
but a true friend
sticks closer than
one's nearest kin.*

PROVERBS 18:24

*Not to us, O LORD,*
*not to us, but to your name*
*we give glory.*

*from* PSALM 115:1

*How very good*
*and pleasant it is*
*when kindred live together*
*in unity.*

PSALM 133:1

*I will sing*
*to the LORD,*
*because he has dealt*
*bountifully with me.*

PSALM 13:6

*O LORD my God,*
*I will give thanks to you*
*forever.*

PSALM 30:12